Why Do Children Lie?

ENCOURAGING
HONESTY IN
CHILDREN

Abimbola
Olayinka

WHY DO CHILDREN LIE?

Copyright © Abimbola Olayinka, 2020

All rights reserved.

ISBN: 978-978-983-420-4

Edited, Designed & Published in Nigeria by
TEBEBA Global Publishing Ltd.

AUTHOR'S CONTACT:
abimbolaolayinka@galparentingplace.com
galparenting@gmail.com

PUBLISHER'S CONTACT:
www.tebeba.com
Tebebapublishing@gmail.com

DEDICATION

This book is dedicated to my loving mum
who taught me contentment in living a simple and peaceful
life, and my loving sister who thought me the true meaning
of friendship. Can you both hear me in heaven?

I love you loads and I will continue to preach the
gospel of peace that you both held so dearly.

Peace starts with me.

CONTENTS

Introduction

> "
>
> What it's like to be a
> parent: it's one of the hardest
> things you'll ever do, but in
> exchange, it teaches you the
> meaningof unconditional love.
>
> ~ **Nicholas Sparks**
>
> "

Why do children lie? Across the globe, this is one of those enduring heartfelt questions on the minds of parents, teachers, guardians, and caregivers. As the world evolves, it seems as if children are getting better at lying. Parents are therefore growing increasingly confused as to why this is so, and what to do about it.

As a parent and an advocate of effective and peaceful parenting, I have come to know more parents who are eager to identify the root cause of lying in children. I understand the plight of these parents. After all, I am a parent too. I also happen to know that this is not a local issue that affects one social group or the other; it is a universal problem in parenting.

The ease with and the extent to which children lie has left psychological scars on most of the parents I have worked with. As a parent, you want to know why your children find it difficult to trust you with the truth. As a teacher, you want to know why your students lie at every turn. As a caregiver or guardian, you want to know why your ward prefers to tell lies. Your apprehension is understandable, especially when you think you have provided the right atmosphere for such a child. I know the depth of your concerns and the many nights you have spent pondering on this problem.

Therefore, I have written this book to help you solve this puzzle and overcome the challenges associated with it. This book, I guarantee, will help you understand the fundamental truths about children, the lies they tell, the various forms of it, underlying reasons for it, and what you need to do to guard against lying. It is therefore expected that you would have gained an in-depth knowledge on how to manage lying as exhibited by children.

More importantly, you will get to know how you directly or indirectly influence the tendency for your child or ward to lie.

Good luck!

THE
PSYCHOLOGY
OF LIES

"Be aware of false
knowledge; it is more
dangerous than ignorance."

~ George Bernard Shaw

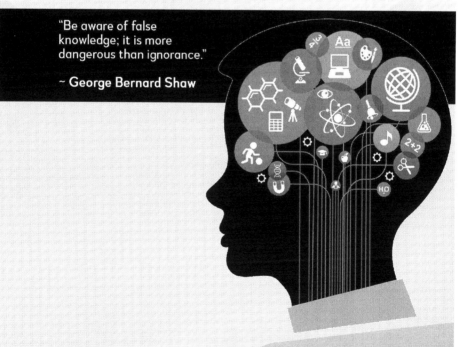

L ying is likely the most prevalent trait that you can find in growing children. This element is present in every child, irrespective of age or gender. Many people think that children are prone to lying on account of the different backgrounds or environments within which they grow. This is not entirely true. Lying in children has nothing to do with geographical borders. It is not a function of the child's race, family or social background. Every child is likely to lie at some point or the other.

Some parents I have worked with have concluded that their financial or social status is responsible for the lies their children tell. I can understand this thought process. However, lying in children is not built on financial situations. That you always provide what your child asks for does not mean they will never tell a lie. That you cannot afford luxury for your child also does not automatically imply that your child will always lie. Your status in the society has nothing to do with lying tendencies in your child.

I want you to understand that it is not all on you as a parent. If your child is determined to lie, they will. So, do not be too hard on yourself if you have tried everything within your power to make your child tell you the truth to no avail.

Lying is Developmentally Normal for Children

Every parent who is raising a child knows that physical and mental growth is healthy and normal in children. What they don't know is that lying is not only beneficial and normal in growing children, but also a part of this healthy mental growth. This is an unusual truth, but the truth, nonetheless. It is as true as the fact that four out of five children will lie at one point or the other.

Lying is extremely healthy for children of all ages. This is one of the findings reported by Talwar and Lee after carrying out an experiment on children. (Talwar & Lee, 2008, p. 879)

The experiment was comparatively simple: children between ages 3 and 8 years were told not to peek at a toy. However, most of the children peeked at the toy, and then denied doing so when questioned. Interestingly, a sort of divide was noticed among the children whereas some of them could not perfectly hold on to the lie they told and made mistakes in covering up others held on to the lies. What became obvious from the study is that children's ability to maintain their lies seems to be related to their moral evaluations. Thus, social and cognitive factors may play an important role in children's lie-telling abilities.

The pinch of the whole research is this; if your child is two, three, four, or seven, and is already lying, you should relax. This is quite normal. It doesn't imply that the child would grow up to be a habitual liar. It's all just growing up.

So, the next time your child tells you a lie, do not fret. Do not get worked up. Do not feel bitter and don't be disturbed. What you are witnessing is relatively healthy and a phase in child development. In fact, all children go through similar developmental stages. You, however, have to be observant when you notice manipulative lies during this developmental phase.

Children Test and Establish Boundaries with Lies

At this point, you may want to ask about children who lie habitually. This too is developmentally normal (Xu et al., 2010, p. 593). The truth is, lying helps your child test the boundaries between fiction and certainty. Children have a wild imagination and love to find out the limits of fiction and the border of truth. They want to be sure of what is going on around them and to eliminate every form of doubt. Their minds develop as they grow. Therefore, they tend to explore their minds to see how things and imaginations occur in them.

Now, am I trying to defend lying in children? Of course, not. My objective is to help you understand that when kids lie, they are usually trying to establish boundaries in order to be able to protect themselves or someone they love.

One other thing you should know is that your children want to know how you or other people think and behave. To them, everyone around them should think and act like them. So, as they develop and realise that their thought patterns are different from yours, they test you with some lies to reveal more of you to them.

It is Okay to Worry

I know it is quite troubling if you discover that your child lies. It's very typical to think that they might become habitual liars. In this kind of situation, it is understandable for you to worry just a little bit. After all, you are a parent who is loving and caring towards your child. However, lying in children should not be something that gives you too much concern. Don't forget that it is developmental and normal. So, your concern (as stated earlier) should centre around manipulative lies.

It has been scientifically proven that lying is one of the indications that your child is hitting developmental milestones per time (Talwar & Lee, 2008, p. 879. Social and Cognitive Correlates of Children's Lying Behaviour). This is in tandem with our earlier assertion that as your children develop mentally, they want to know what you think and what your thought pattern is like; they want to know if you feel and see things the same way they do. This could contribute to why they tell lies, and the more reason why you should reduce your worries.

On a side note, there's the problem of pathological lying. Pathological lying is a considerably more profound problem and may be indicative of mental illnesses such as obsessive-compulsive disorder, anxiety disorder, anti-social personality disorder, and *pseudo logia fantastic* (Serota, K. B. & Levine, T. R. (2015, p. 157). When a child has any of these, medical attention must be sought before the condition grows worse. However, in the absence of any of these or other medical conditions, parents can rest easy, knowing that lying is a phase of life that helps children adjust, test, and appreciate life happenings. Besides, lying affords children the ability to explore their minds creatively.

All in all, lies that tend to be manipulative and pathological in nature must be quickly identified by parents. Their diversities and how it affects children would be investigated in the next chapter.

THE DIVERSITY OF LIES

"A lie is a lie. A white lie is a lie. A half-truth is a lie. A lie by omission is a lie..."

~ Smriti Sinha

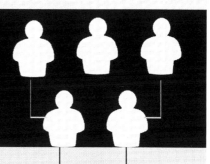

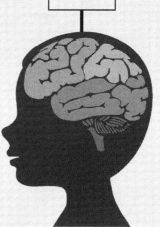

In the previous chapter, we established certain facts, including that lying in children is a natural part of their mental and developmental growths. In this chapter, we shall dive a little deeper into the subject.

What are the various lies that children tell? How do you know that a lie is problematic: that it is not the result of developmental traits? How do you know when children become manipulative with lies? What are the red signals to watch out for in a lying child?

Research shows that there are different types of lies that children tell from time to time. Although a lie is a lie, the intensity of these lies and the intentionality behind them varies. To be able to deal accordingly with the different types of lies, you must be able to understand lies in their different forms. Doing this will help you to identify what type of lie your child engages in and why. Of course, I expect that at the end of this chapter, you would understand exactly what goes through the mind of your child which would assist you to react accordingly. And if your child requires medical assistance, you will be better prepared to appropriately handle it.

Types of Manipulative Lie

Lying comes in different forms in children of all ages. Some lies are a result of medical and mental illness in children. This type can only be altered by medical intervention. However, other forms of lie do not require any medical attention. These are the most typical forms of lying in children. Then there are manipulative lies, which are lies which children tell in other to manipulate the minds of others into believing them, just to suit themselves.

This chapter would therefore examine seven different types of lies that children tell and the occasions that surround them.

Lying by Mistake
Lying by mistake is a form of lie which a child commits by error. The child, in this case, does not lie intentionally. He believes that he is truthful, but in the real sense, it is a lie.

For example, if you ask your child the number of students in the class, he could say ten. To him, this is correct because he counted ten. However, this might be untrue and therefore, a lie. Imagine that one child in the class had bent down to lace his shoes and was left out when your child counted. So, the lie is unintentional and therefore a mistake. Quite pitifully, many parents are not aware that children can tell lies by mistake. They often believe that most time a child lies intentionally. However, this is not always the case.

Lying by Omission

This type of lie happens when a part of the truth is being consciously omitted. It is unlike the previous where the lie is unintentional. When your child tells you a lie by omission, they know and are fully aware that they have left out a portion of the truth.

For instance, you got home after the day's work, and you realised that your fridge had stopped working. So, you decided to ask your son what happened. He may then say, "Mum, I was just passing by, and I realised that the fridge has stopped working." That would be lying by omission, if in the real sense, he was passing by and mistakenly did something that caused the fridge to stop working.

Most times, children who lie by omission know what they are doing. They know the consequence of telling the truth. They know your behaviour and the way you will probably react if they dare speak the whole truth. Thus, lying protects them so they lie.

Likewise, children could lie to protect other people around them. They could go as far as telling a lie in other to cover up for a friend's behaviour that can lead to punishment or a more severe consequence. They could tell a lie by omission in other to protect their sibling who has done wrong from the aftermath of their decisions. These cases exemplify lying by omission by telling a part of the truth or nothing at all.

Lie by Restructuring

This is a type of lie in which the truth is being restructured intentionally to suit the scope of the liar. For instance, if a child is asked, "Why is your sister crying?" and he goes on to say, "Mummy, she kicked me, slapped me, tore my book, and I just pushed her slightly." Already, he knows that was not how it happened. To save himself, he had to reconstruct the whole scenario to influence you and suit his feelings using lying by reconstruction.

Lying by Denial

This is often regarded as an outright repudiation of the truth. Here, the child does not omit or restructure anything; what he does is deny the obvious truth that you have set before him. No matter the amount of evidence that you have against that child committing such an act, he would deny it. Usually, children do this because they do not want to own up to their actions and take responsibility.

Lying by Minimisation

Has your child ever responded to your question by reducing the efficacy and effect of her action in her response? That is minimisation: a form of lying where the child speaks the truth but removes the intensity with which it happened. In other words, they simplify their actions and make them appear ordinary as if any form of punishment would be too much.

Children would sometimes tell lies in this way to appeal to their consciousness because they feel remorse for what they have done.

Even adults use this to cover up sometimes. Let me give an illustration.

Let us say your child just called another child 'stupid' in your presence, and you decided to scold him right there. He could attempt to excuse himself from the punishment by trying to minimise what he has said. He could say, "Oh, I didn't mean that, I was just joking." This is a lie by minimisation because he meant what he has said.

Lying by Fabrication

Children often fabricate imaginary scenes in their head. They want to tell you things that do not exist, so they go ahead to create it in their made-up minds. This is lying since what they are saying is false.

Let's say you ask your child how he's doing at school: instead of saying, "Oh, I'm doing very well" or "I'm not doing very well," your child might go on blabbing about how he performed so well in school that he became the envy of others. He could even create an imaginary picture of how his teacher told him to stand up in class for other pupils to clap for him. That is a fabricated lie because it didn't happen.

He was only trying to create a soothing mental instance. He just wanted you to see how amazing he can be in school. If fabricating a lie would make him achieve that, then that seems okay for him.

I have seen children who would tell their parents that they have made their bed whereas they haven't. They would even go as far as testing their imagination by telling you the colours of the beddings and the pillow and how perfectly such a colour looks. Getting to the room, you will find that to be nothing but a false story.

Lying by Exaggeration

Lying by exaggeration usually occurs in children when they are trying to paint a picture so well for you to believe. They know if they say it in its simplicity, you might not take it as serious as they want. So, they go ahead to add other elements into it to make it believable.

If your child wants you to give him some money for school, he could give you a reported speech of what the teacher said would happen if he fails to do so. True, the teacher might have said, "I will punish you if you don't come along with your money." In a bid to make you pay quickly, your child may exaggerate the teacher's speech.

He could say that the teacher was going to beat him and take him around the whole school if he does not pay up. He could even add that the teacher would send him out of the class all through the day. That is an exaggeration, and it's a form of lying.

These are the different forms of lying, especially by children. I imagine that your mind has begun to ponder which form of lying your child is inclined to. I also hope that you have realised that children are smart enough to form mental pictures in their heads so they can protect themselves and their loved ones. This understanding of the types of lies that children tell should help you understand the reasons behind a lying child and how it could be managed.

In the next chapter, we will settle on the core; why exactly do children lie?

WHY DO CHILDREN LIE?

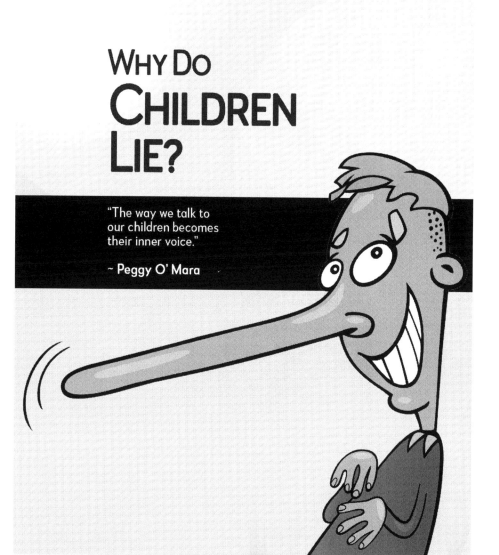

"The way we talk to
our children becomes
their inner voice."

~ Peggy O' Mara

We have already established the most obvious forms of lying that children resort to. Now, we shall turn our minds to understanding why children lie in the first place.

It is possible that you have wondered why children often fail to outrightly speak the truth. Is it an automatic fault built into humanity, or something even more extraordinary? It actually revolves around the way children think, what goes on in their minds, and how they perceive things or events. What you must realise above all else is that there is a rational and practical purpose behind children lying. So, rest your mind the devil is not whispering into their ears.

There is a Purpose

Let us begin by reiterating what a lie is. There is no universally accepted definition of lying. However, the most basic and conventional definition. Of lie was seen in Isenberg (1963), it covered all the basis with the notion that, "A lie is a statement made by one who does not believe it with the intention that someone else shall be led to believe it." In other words, to lie is to make a false statement to another person, with the intention of having the other person believe that statement to be true. So, what exactly drives this intention in children?

The following are some of the more common factors that inspire lying in children.

Getting their Wishes

Most of the time, children tell lies to get what they want or to get out of something that they do not want to do. A child who wants to eat candy before brushing his teeth will likely lie and claim that his teeth are brushed because he knows that the only way you will give him candy is by having him first brush his teeth. It is relatively straightforward.

Instincts

Children, like adults, have instincts that drive their actions most of the time. When you accuse a child of an offence, the instinct to defend himself could motivate lying to protect himself from dire consequences. Besides, his instincts could hint him that it is safer to tell lies than to tell the truth, pointing to him that if he denies the act, he would obviously avoid further questions in relation to that situation. After all, you won't ask him why he did it when he tells you that he didn't do anything. So, lying could be instinctive.

At other times, a child would often tell lies so as to avoid the consequences of an offence that he has committed. For a child who you have set rules and the resulting consequence for, upon violation of such regulations, telling lies always appears a safe getaway from punishment, which is equally intuitive.

As a quick plus, children also tell lies to test their parents; there is no helping it. They instinctively want to try to get into your head and see what sort of reasoning is right there. So, they would often test you with a lie one time and again. When they do this, they usually are not trying to hurt you or anything, they are just trying to observe your beliefs, opinions, emotional displays and reactions towards them.

Unbelief

Let's experiment a bit. Cast your mind back to twenty years ago or more and recall an incident when you were wrongly accused of a negative behaviour. How did you feel about that? What was your reaction then? This is what children feel sometimes.

Children are aware that their parents do not always believe them. They know that telling the truth does not immediately change whatever conclusions their parents make about an issue. These children have grown to understand that daddy and mummy are usually impatient when it comes to such matters. So, they lie away, and continue to lie and lie and lie.

Children can read body language perfectly well. So, they know when you believe everything they are saying, and when you do not believe one bit of it. You do not have to say so, they can see it all.

Every child wants to be believed, especially when they tell the truth about a matter. Whether they are wrong or right, they want you first to pay attention and listen to what they have to say. When you refuse to and insist that they "cut the long story short and admit that you did this," lying becomes a refuge.

Lack of Trust

Lying could also be regarded to as a deliberate incorrect response to a question. In other words, an act or inquiry must have taken place before a child chooses to lie as an option. A question must have been asked or an act must have been committed before a child decides to lie. We have built the terms around this understanding of action and reaction. The practice of communicating lie is what is called lying, while the person who conveys the lie is called a liar.

Drawing from my experience with my clients, I have found out that a few children tell lies because they don't trust their listeners/audience. Thus, if your child tells you some blatant lie, it may be that he doesn't trust you with the truth.

There are two significant reasons why we do not trust people: First, because we don't know them and secondly, because we know them very well. Children are no different. These two factors shape and influence the decisions of children per time. When you see a child who tells a lie so well, his decision to lie might have been caused by the adequate or the inadequate knowledge that he has of his parents, teachers, guardians or caregiver.

The Fear of Punishment

The fear of punishment is another reason many children don't trust their parents with the truth. If every bitter revelation is accompanied by a resounding knock on the head, a child may find that not saying the truth, that is, lying, is a much safer route.

For most parents, punishment is usually the first response to a wrong committed by a child. Such parents go the extra mile of scolding and beating up a child because of what he has done wrong. In truth, punishing a child by inflicting pain through beating can cause physical injuries to the health and emotional wellbeing of that child. To avoid this consequence, your child may lie.

Do not get me wrong. I am not excusing bad behaviour. No! It is indispensable for parents to discipline their children, as this is one of the corrective tools of parenting. However, discipline and punishment are not the same things, neither do they have the same effects. One is a corrective measure to put a child on the right path whereas the other harms the child and prevents you from earning trust.

To Make Stories Beautiful
As stated earlier, children have very wild imaginations. Their minds are thoroughly capable of creating exciting wonders about life occurrences, and that is why many children love to replay whatever they see on the TV screen. It occurs first in their minds, and then, they act it out. Having a replay helps them to have a better understanding of the story. Also, they would be more conscious of such reports and would always look for an opportunity to make use of it in real life. Children also have a way of editing the scenes of these movies as a part of the creative

thinking in them.

Constant practice in this regard helps them to develop their mind, to the point that they can create stories even when there are no stories. This ability is what they channel, and unfortunately abuse when they lie. It isn't a deliberate scam; they just want to create a beautiful scene for you. Of course, children know that their parents would prefer to hear good and positive stories. So, they give you well-crafted lie in excellent and positive packages.

Children are susceptible to the needs of people around them, including their parents. When they find out that good and beautiful stories make you comfortable as a parent, they won't hesitate to provide you with one. They hate to make you feel bad. For this reason, they can go as far as fabricating a lie in other to construct the kind of story that you would want. When children tell lies like this, it is often on account of what they have witnessed over time from their parents, and what they have been led to believe.

To Seek Attention

Parenting is not an easy task. It is a responsibility that is well able to end lives if adequate preparations were not made beforehand. I understand that you are doing your very possible best to cater for the children and the family at large. Well done! Only great parents willingly go through daily parenting stress. Did you know, however, that being a child is just as demanding?

You have probably forgotten what it was to be a child. Allow me to remind you. A child always needs his parents. It does not matter the kind of work that you do or the level of stress that you are going through, your children will always need you. They would regularly seek out your attention and interest and would rarely let go. Take that attention and interest, and they will tell enough lies to win back your attention.

There is no selfishness in the several demands of children. If you are the type of parent who does not pay attention to these peculiar needs of your children, be ready to hear all sorts of lies. If you don't take adequate time to be with your child, you may find out that such a child might begin to lie to you. That's one way you contribute to this whole thing.

In the next chapter, we will look into how parents can be a significant influence and a party to the lying tendency in their children.

PARENT INFLUENCE:

PARTIES TO LIE IN CHILDREN

"Parents are the ultimate role models for children. Every word, every moment and action affect. No other person or outside force has a greater influence on a child than a parent."

~ Bob Keeshan

Parenting is one of the most influential jobs that you can ever have in the world, regardless of whether the world bows at your feet or doesn't know you at all. You are a person of influence as long as you are a parent.

From the womb to their cradle, even to their adulthood, the effects of parents on their children are simply phenomenal. No other group compares to them, not even teachers from the school, relatives from a distant land, or guardians in the society.

You are almost certainly the first person your children ever had contact with. Their earliest impressions come from you, from seeing, knowing and understanding you, as well as how you do things. In fact, you are simply the foundation of your children. That's a profound weight of influence.

It is possible that you are ignorant of the effects that your actions, behaviour and disposition have on your children. Whatever act or traits that your child would grow up with began with/from you. This is one of the hacks of parenting and a reliable underpinning for ensuring positive character in your children.

So, a few things you must take to heart.

It Begins with the Parents

To begin with, the ability to bend the truth is a developmental milestone. It is really no different from walking and talking. The results of a practical research led by Kang Lee (a Professor of Psychology at the University of Toronto) and Victoria Talwar (in 2008) have shown that lying is a proof that your children are hitting their developmental milestones. In other words, you need not worry.

When you should worry as a parent, if ever, is when your child begins to lie with deep intention to manipulate. Interestingly, however, parents are usually one of the significant causes behind their children's manipulative lies. In fact, I will go even further to state that for almost every manipulative lie told by a child, there is a line that connects to parental action and involvement.

I earlier outlined the influences that you have on your children as they grow. They can either be positive or negative in nature. Lying by manipulation is a negative influence on your child. When children inherit a legacy of lying, it is expected that they bear it to fruition.

Some manipulative lies in children have their bedrock in parents and the psychosocial environment of the child. For example, why do children lie to their parents when they want to get something from them? Easy, children know that their parents want to hear a smooth talk or nothing at all. So even when there is no tangible reason for a request, he might tell a lie to manipulate you, and then get what he wants.

None of this is mere speculation. There are numerous research works and findings that back up the fact that lies in children start directly from their home, right under the watch of their parents. A recent and notable study is one undertaken by Professor Kang Lee, at the University of Toronto's Ontario Institute for Studies in Education (Santos, R. M., Zanette, S., Kwok, S. M., Heyman, G. D, & Lee, K. (2017). The study did not only show that parents play a monumental role in the lying tendencies of their children, but also the existence of ripple effects that connects the attitudes of parents to their children, that is, in both child and adulthood.

Suffice to state that lying is a part of a child's mental development. It can also be a negative influence posed at a child as a result of the psychosocial environment of the child.

Be at Peace with Yourself

One of the primary reasons children tell manipulative lies, as we have discussed earlier, is that often times children do not seem to trust their parents. Trust me, this can't be truer. If your children cannot trust you with their words and confessions, then get ready for daily rides of lies.

Your children need to find you worthy of their security and confidence as a parent. They need to know that they can trust you with the truth. What is worrisome is that if your child continually lives in fear of you and does not trust you, the chances are that the child may find it difficult to open up to you with ease going forward.

Do you see how the ball is in your court?

Take time to consider; do you trust yourself? Do you trust your decisions and your actions? Can you maintain calm when faced with ugly truths from your children? How well can you control your anger and emotions? If you make a decision not to react badly, do you trust yourself not to?

Peace has always been the language that holds a family together. When you see a family that is at the edge of falling apart and needs to be saved, simply introduce peaceful strategies of keeping a home together to the leaders in the family. It will amaze you how things will turn around for good.

For every family that will continually ride off the wings of peace, note that peace has to start with the individuals involved in the family. The father has to be at peace with himself before he can be at peace with other members of the family; likewise, the mother and the children. As an advocate of peaceful parenting, I know this well because I have preached, practised, and taught other parents peaceful parenting over the years, and the positive results are evident.

The truth is that your children cannot be at peace with you when you are not at peace with yourself.

Attaining internal peace with oneself is achievable through deliberate and intentional efforts. In the absence of these, peace may elude us.

To me, I would say this is more of achieving peace with yourself to enable you achieve peace with others. How do you respond to unpleasant issues? Are you full of abusive and vulgar words? Do you rain derogatory comments on people when their behaviours and actions become unpalatable?

Your children can see all these when you do them. They can see that their beloved mummy just lashed out at someone with her words. They can hear you raising your voice over the phone while speaking with your secretary. They can see these, and even though they are kids, they are smart enough to see these as your negative traits. Because you are an automatic role model to them, they may likely pick up these negative traits and exhibit them to you and other people.

Being at peace with yourself essentially explains whether you are capable of regulating your emotions or not. Negative and positive emotions are part of human wiring. There is no one without emotional extremities. Handling these extremities is how you win peace for yourself and your family.

Mindset

Your mind plays a vital role in what, how, and why you do things.

This is why you must guard your mind and shield yourself and your children from emotional and psychological impairment or injury.

Punishment by beating is a limiting belief in parenting which resonates around inflicting pain as way of correction. Of course, we are often aware that mistakes do happen and that they are not age sensitive. But most times we overreact because of our default programming. After the impulse action, there is a tendency for you to calm down and feel sober for the unnecessary action.

What about the aftermath? Do you apologise to your child once you realise you've gone overboard? For someone with an empowering mind set, apologising won't be difficult. However, it will be pretty difficult when the mindset is laced with disempowering beliefs. Again, this is how limiting belief in parenting works.

Let me add here that there is nothing wrong with you apologising to your children. In fact, it's a beautiful thing to do as a parent. It does not mean that you are weak or less of a parent. But rather, it shows that you are able to teach that child that mistakes happen in life, and reparation is critical. Besides, apologizing to your children gets them on your side, shows them that you aren't infallible, and it equally aids in building trust.

If you can impress just this mindset into your children, they will become more open to you. They will share their deeply held truths with you and come to depend on your opinions and endorsement.

One of the reasons for lying in children is the fact that parents expect perfect behaviours and conduct from them. For fear of the emotional rage and punishment from their parents, children often tell manipulative lies. However, when parents maintain their inner peace and manage their emotions appropriately, they increase the level of trust that their children have in them.

In the next chapter, we will outline how to deal with lying in children.

Dealing With Lies In Children

> "By loving them more than their abilities, we show our children that they are much more than the sum of their accomplishments."
>
> ~ Eileen Kennedy- Moore

For every challenge life presents, there is usually a remedy. However, the ability to discern the right remedy for the appropriate challenge is the deciding factor. Imagine a challenge of bodily sickness, knowing whether to use antimalarial remedies or antibiotics is tantamount to knowing how to save a life. This is to reiterate that there is a remedy for almost every malady. Lying in children is no different.

As peculiar as the problem of lying in children is, there are more than a few ways of resolving it. However, each solution has its effects which is why it is super important that you understand your children and then urge them appropriately to achieve your aim.

How to Deal with Lies

Strengthen your emotional connection
Emotional connection (or attachment) is a term that describes a

special bond between two people which is generally both powerful and enduring. In recent years, this term has been used to describe the relationship between infants and their mothers (Koulenti, T. & Anastassiou-Hadjicharalambous, X. (2011).

This connection occurs naturally, but it must be deliberately cultivated and nurtured, or you risk losing it. This is why it is vital that you, the parent, make conscious efforts towards strengthening your emotional connection with your children.

The cuddles, kisses, walks that you share with your children are simple ways of bonding with them. Every random hug is very magical and strikes a deep chord in your children. So, hug them and strengthen the bonds.

Create a rapport by listening

One way to strengthen the emotional connection between you and your children is rapport which comes from listening to them. You must be able to have significant interactions with them. Do you make out time to chat with your children? Many parents think that their children are too young for dialogue, but this isn't true. Listening to them is a principal element in understanding them, strengthening bonds, and getting them to trust you.

Creating rapport with your children also involves patience from your end. This could mean that you have to sit or stay where you are for several minutes because you are listening to your children. You must be patient with your children to such a degree that you can listen to them with rapt attention. Doing so allows you into their world, and you'll be amazed by what you find.

Spend quality time with them

Patience is an essential virtue of humanity and this is usually expressed by time spent. It is also one of the best gifts and heritage that you can offer to your children. You don't need to have many luxuries. However, when you invest your time into your children, you have planted a permanent and ever-growing seed that would grow to strengthen your emotional connection for life.

In spending time with your children, the quality of time (rather than the quantity) is what matters. A lot of parents have mixed this up. They assume that spending time with children means just staying at home with them. There is a difference between being physically present and spending quality time and being physically present but emotionally absent.

Quality time involves intentionally taking time out and dedicating it to your children. It involves moments that you spend talking with them passionately, playing with them intimately, and helping them out with schoolwork. You are not spending quality time with your children if while talking to them you still go ahead to engage in social activities on your phone. If other things distract you from focusing on them when you are home, then that is quantity, and not quality time.

Spending quality time with your children comes with a price that you must be ready and willing to pay. It means that you have to prioritise activities at that time. It means that you are prepared to close your eyes to what is happening on social media, that even your friends who want to gist might not be able to reach you at that time. Why? Because you have dedicated that time to be with your children.

Use such dedicated times to have meaningful conversations with your children. Ask about their school activities, play games together and tell stories and folk tales. Share with them your own childhood stories and experiences. Laugh with them and let them relate and talk with you freely. Ask about their friends and teachers and show them that you care. This is how you strengthen emotional bonds.

If you can take proper stock and control of your time when relating with your children, you will earn their trust and strengthen your emotional connection with them. This way, you would be able to reduce the conditions that enables lying.

Remember that a child who feels loved and cared for is unlikely to lie manipulatively. Even the prospect of discipline may not be enough to deter him from telling you the truth when he does something wrong.

Listen to them
You equally strengthen your emotional connection with your child by practicing effective listening. You are not listening if your child is talking to you, and you are distracted by your phone. You are not listening if your child is talking to you, and your attention is focused on the TV. Effective listening involves maintaining eye contact with your child when your child is speaking. It means that you are displaying the right gesture and body language to show that you are following. Sometimes, you might even need to repeat their words to prove that you are genuinely listening to them.

Don't be judgemental

Being judgmental is easy, and it is one of the primary causes of disconnect between a parent and a child. It is effortless to see what other people have done wrong and quickly give a verdict about it. Even as parents, we sometimes find it easy to point out the mistakes of our children and express dissatisfaction. Even though it is important to point out mistakes of erring children, while doing this it is imperative that the circumstances which surrounded the child's decision making process be put into perspective.

Your actions may be the result of your disempowering beliefs about parenting, which may have a negative effect on your emotional bond with your child. So, the next time you want to be judgmental, take a long pause. Reprocess what your child has said or done. That way, you will find a better way to express your feelings.

Don't tell them, show them!

Children learn rapidly. They quickly absorb traits and characters that they have witnessed over time. You may believe that training your child involves using only verbal corrective measures and guidance. This is part of but not the only or most effective way of nurturing kids. Our children watch us and everyone else around them. They may not show it, but I assure you they are watching and learning much of what they see you say and do. Just like the saying, "children see, children do."

Children instinctively want you to show them how to live, and not with words. They want to SEE HOW in your own life. Your children are (most of the time) modified versions of you. Therefore, if there is a certain way that you would love them to behave and act, show them. If you want them to be loving and caring, be loving and caring. Give them the kisses and the hugs that they need.

When you do this, you strengthen your emotional connection with your children because you are practising what you are preaching and not confusing them with your words against your actions.

Let your discipline be kind

I have explained this earlier, but I will stress the point here again. Discipline is very different from punishment. To discipline your child is to use corrective measures, it does not involve inflicting physical pain on that child by way of beating. It does not include raining down derogative and abusive words. Discipline is a critical tool in parenting. As a parent or guardian you cannot exempt discipline when training your children. Doing so implies over-indulging them, and this is not wise. However, first, understand the concept of discipline.

Let me highlight a few things about the term and idea of discipline.

The word discipline is derived from the Latin word "discipulus," which loosely translates as "to learn." Explicitly, discipline is a way of life that is in accordance with certain rules and regulations. It is a sort of self-control, restraint, and strength of will, all of which are reflected in public actions. This control is not forced upon the individual but flows out from within. Thus, discipline is more than mere submission to authority, but an attitude that is both natural and cultivated (Essay on Discipline: Definition,

Concept, Components and Principles, 2020.)

When your children err, discipline them in a very firm but kind manner. Not that a child spills oil, and you ask him to kneel for ten hours. Or maybe your child uses vulgar words, and you refuse to feed him all through the day. That's too much! The level of discipline must correspond to the offence that was committed.

Furthermore, discipline involves you showing and making the child realize what they did wrong. If you discipline your child and he cannot afterwards point at something he has learned from it, then, your child was punished and not disciplined.

Note that true discipline requires consistency. This means you will most likely have to correct a child again and again for the same thing. This is normal, they are still children and are still learning. You can take away certain privileges, set reasonable rules and boundaries, state and set up reasonable consequences for negative behaviour, and follow through.

Every child wants to obey and behave appropriately, especially when they know and trust you. So, be patient while correcting them. This way, you can be a respected parent and one worthy of trust. Meanwhile, your emotional connection with them is being strengthened through the process.

Accept them

One of the ways to create an emotional connection with your children is to accept them the way they are. If you have two or more kids, you must understand that each one is unique in character, emotion, and intellect. They are fashioned and wired differently from one another. So, you should not compare them with each other or other people's children. In behaviour and academic performance, don't make comparisons. Accept them first, then nurture them in whatever area they are lacking.

If you always compare your kids with others, you will hurt them emotionally. Soon enough, they will strive to impress you which might include some levels of manipulative lies.

If your children have not done well and you want them to rise up to a particular standard, call them and speak calmly to them. Explain to them and make them see the reasons why they need to improve. Ask them questions about their poor performance and be willing to encourage them and also let them know that they can improve.

Play with them

Playing is essential in raising children and in strengthening emotional connection with them. Your children would love you more and always tell their friends that you are fantastic if you always play with them. It's okay if you don't have all the time to play outside and even inside with them, but you can still be intentional about creating a special playtime out of your busy schedule for them. Spend quality time with them by taking a stroll or going shopping together. Once in a while, you can decide to take them out for lunch or dinner, or even make special meals for them. Watch an exciting movie that they love with them, laugh, and learn together.

Let them make decisions

Mistakes are unavoidable for adults as well as children, it isn't something they can help, but it is as a result of their curiosity. You cannot isolate children from their growth. How will they make brilliant decisions if they have not made some mistakes before time? How will they live life graciously if you don't allow them to go through the process of life? Even in their errors, be calm and ensure you are neither critical nor judgmental. Your children want you to be parents who can trust them even when they fall a bit short of that trust.

In my relationship with children over the years, I found out that they often want to make decisions by themselves. When they grow to a particular stage, they want you to trust them with their decision making. That's why you will see a child climb on the sofa and jump to the ground from that high pedestal. Sometimes you will see them play with some object that can hurt them. This is where parents get extra protective. Of course, you wouldn't want your children to fall, fail, or get hurt. However, this zealous overprotection can be risky as it could deprive them of certain things, including their quest to be confident, resilient and fearless.

I am not saying that you should watch while your child gets hurt while playing. I am only saying that you should grant them some liberty to try out some things. As much as you are protective of them, avoid the extremity of being overprotective. Usually, we learn through our mistakes. So, let them explore and be creative in their minds. Safety comes first, that's true. Therefore, if they must handle some objects or appliances, let it be with your supervision. If you can sometimes trust them with their decisions by allowing them to take the lead, happy will they be, and your bond with them will wax stronger.

Encourage their small wins

You love and yearn for encouragement, don't you? Imagine you have accomplished something of note, and then your spouse refuses to say a word about it. Imagine that nobody recognizes how awesome you are, even when you have achieved only a little. How do you feel then? Your children are no different.

As a parent, make it a point of duty to appreciate and encourage your children. You do not need to wait until they do spectacular things before you cheer them. That little increase in their grade performance deserves a cheer from you. Encourage them in their small wins. Don't just see the things that they do as expected and overlook them. That's not good enough. Even when you expect so much from them, still appreciate and encourage the little that they have done. As long as you are supportive and fully involved in their academics and other things of interest to them, the sky will be a starting point because of your backing.

If you make strengthening your emotional connection with your children a daily task, you won't only be an effective parent, but one with a positive influence on children. As a result, your children will gradually come to see you as someone they can talk to and relate with. In the process, they may never have to manipulate you in any way.

Having discussed the ways to deal with lies in children, we must proceed to establish the strategies to make you curb the acts of lying in your child or ward. It is not enough to only deal with the lies. We must begin to break those cycles from becoming habitual in our children.

All aboard the next chapter!

THWARTING
THE
CIRCLE

"It is easier to build
strong children than to
repair broken men."

~ Frederick Douglass

Children are like seeds, and their development is no different from the growth of a tree. For any tree to blossom and flourish, a conscious and targeted effort must be directed towards factors that might hinder its growth. Same applies to lying in children. A complete quashing of the cycle of manipulative lies in your child would require deliberate, dedicated, and consistent efforts.

Lying, as we established in the previous chapter, starts from the way you handle the lies that accompany child development and your attitude around your child. Therefore, the process of uprooting the stems of lying in your children also begins with you.

How to Break the Cycle of Lying

Practice what you preach

Say what you mean and mean what you say: it is that simple. Desist from saying one thing and doing another. You cannot stop your child's manipulative lies if you exhibit same. It will not help the situation one bit. As a parent, be deliberate about not telling lies around your children. The little ones are watching and absorbing all you do.

Parents tell different lies in the presence of their kids. You might hear a parent who is on the phone claiming that he is almost at the meeting point when he is clearly at home. These children are neither blind nor deaf. They can hear and see you lie.

Your lies might be justifiable, but no reason is good enough for you to lie, especially in the presence of your children. No matter the explanation you give them, it cannot rule out the fact that you have broken the same rule you set.

It is easy for parents to set specific rules to be followed by their children. However, never forget that you must follow those rules yourself. Remember, show them, don't only tell them. If you instruct your children never to stay out late, don't stay out late too. If you urge them to desist from lying, desist from lying. There are no white lies, a lie is a lie. This is the understanding of children. So, use the energy you might spend in defending your actions to correct your actions. You are the first model that your children have in this world, so you have no other choice than to be a good one.

As a role model, you are expected to model the right behaviour and values into them, including positive values such as honesty and truthfulness. Practice the simple acts of telling the truth, especially when it's not convenient. If you don't want your children to lie, don't make a practice of lying.

Be approachable

As a 21st Century parent, I understand that there is pressure from work and other activities and obligations. However, you can work around busy schedules and handle these pressures if you want to. So, have your emotions (and emotional pressures) under control, and relate with your children. They are not the source of our problems at work, so it will be unfair to transfer the aggression to them.

There are a lot of parents who are guilty in this regard, who push everyone, including their children away. Their children often find it hard to approach them for a chitchat not to talk of more demanding things. Because they, like gasoline waiting to explode, are one moment away from shouting and yelling at everyone.

It is understandable that you are going through a hard time, but don't take it out on your children. Don't make them pay for your emotional wreckage. If you need some time to yourself, tell them, and help them understand why. All in all, it is important that you are approachable, even when you aren't in the right frame of mind. How do you do this?

Do not let your emotions control you. Call your children together and tell them you need to be alone for some time. Trust me, they will understand perfectly and behave accordingly. When you have calmed down and are in top condition, you can then return to them. This is the way of peaceful parenting.

Being approachable isn't just theoretical. It is to be practised over and over again by parents at home. If you want your children to talk freely with you and tell you the truth, maintain a posture of approachability. Don't scare them off with glares and glowers. Smile, be welcoming and be mindful of your body language and tone.

Praise honesty

It is not easy for a child to walk up to you to tell you the truth. This takes real courage and a level of connection between you two. When they do, praise them, and commend them for telling the truth. Don't regard it as a normal thing. Every time they open up truthfully to you, let your words and body language show your appreciation.

Be a leader

Aside being a parent to your children, you are also a leader at home. And you are not just any leader, but an exemplary leader. If you must raise award-winning children who are free from the constraints of a manipulative or deceitful lie, your style of leadership is vital. So, what type of leader are you?

John Maxwell, in his book "How to Lead Yourself," explains how leadership is influence; nothing more and nothing less. A leader is someone who knows the way, shows the way and leads the way. He also went further to state the five levels of leadership namely; Position, Permission, Production, People Development and Pinnacle (respect). A parent-leader must move from a place of positional leadership to leadership through respect. Once in a while, ask your children, are you taking instructions from me because I am your parent, or you aspire to be like me when you grow up? (I wish I had the luxury to listen to their responses).

If your children cannot trust your leadership and therefore look outside the home for one, you are no longer in control.

There is a right way to parenting and leadership on the home front. This isn't related to how you were parented, but what you know. Parenting, at the end of the day, does not need to be done alone— it is more than okay to seek professional service.

Let go of anger

If you have residual anger from the bitter experiences of your childhood, don't cuddle it, try to let it go. I know it is tempting to hold on to that anger and pain: don't fall for it. There is only one outcome for it, and that is more anger and pain, as well as harm and damage to your children.

Majority of our parents didn't know any better when they were training us, and that explains how we were treated. Now, we know better. Therefore, should we choose to wallow in pain and the resentment, we could be passing on that same inappropriate training and parenting unto our children. It would be infinitely better to let that pain propel us to do better and be the best parent for our children.

Because you know better, you must let go of the pain of the past so that you can connect emotionally with your children. Just as you were yearning for love during your childhood, your children are also yearning for much more. You must give them your love;

it is within your power to do so.

Do not deny your children the right to evolve and explore. Moving ahead in life is key to your progress as a parent and to the growth of your children. Kindly put in your best to heal from your childhood trauma and find closure or you risk repeating the same cycle of childhood pain and hurt, as you cannot give what you don't have.

Make out time to talk calmly

Make out time to talk calmly about how lying can affect the relationship between yourself and your child, as well as the effect that lies have on the child's relationship with other family members. This is the best way to put things in perspective for your children without having to torture them with harsh whips and harsher words.

You could create a scenario for your child. Turn that power of imagination to your advantage. In this way, you are capturing and helping the child understand the effects of manipulative lies and deceit, especially towards his relationship with others and his self-image.

Let your child know that you
are aware of his lie when he is telling one

This is both instructive and straightforward. Having caught your child, you could say "hey dear, what is wrong today? You are usually honest with me, so why are you being dishonest now? Is there a way to help get the truth out of you?" Refrain from calling your child a 'liar', so you don't reinforce the lies. Otherwise, you risk having him become what you frequently call him: a liar. Instead, gently and lovingly remind him of the positive values of honesty.

Take note that the psychosocial environment of children in the early years go a long way in moulding and shaping their behaviour in adulthood. What your child is today is a seed of what he could become. Be vigilant and careful.

Finally, parents, it is not enough to just know that lying is developmentally normal. Neither is it sufficient to only know ways of dealing with manipulative lies or deceit. Whereas knowing this is important, it is however imperative for you to come to a place of self-awareness as parents to enable you build and become the best foundation for your children. This is how you help them get the best out of life. This is how you thwart the cycle of lying and make the future of your children a little brighter.

Remember, our children watch us for a living.

Conclusion

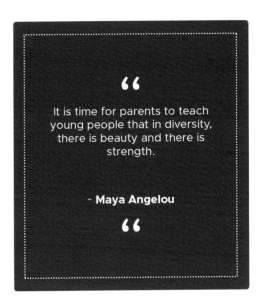

> It is time for parents to teach young people that in diversity, there is beauty and there is strength.
>
> ~ **Maya Angelou**

We have learned quite a bit so far, the foundation and psychology of lying, its different forms, the rationales behind it, the depth of parental influence, and how to deal with it.

Now you understand that it is not enough to be a parent by title alone. You must be a parent who understands the essence of parenthood. You have to learn to be at peace with yourself, which will lead to your emotional stability thus gaining the trust of your children. Do everything within your power to strengthen the emotional connection with your children. If you must raise children who are honest and trustworthy, be approachable and cut them some slack. You can, and so you must.

I agree that raising children isn't as easy as it used to be. In recent times, parenting requires hard work, determination, and resilience. It requires that parents wake up to the responsibilities involved in grooming responsible children who will grow up to be responsible adults. As much as we need time for ourselves to work and rest, we must reach a balance. As long as this balance is reached and children are emotionally connected to their parents, lying manipulatively and dishonesty will lose its hold.

As parents who have unlearned, learned and still relearning from this book, what are the actions and reactions you intend to put a stop to? What will you start to do differently? What areas require improvement? What areas require continuity? Don't hold back. Start now.

Whatever steps you need to take to strengthen your emotional connection with your children, take them now. Whatever adjustments you need to make to be at peace with yourself and also that of your children, kindly make them now.

This is what I have learnt from my many years of peaceful parenting and coaching. If you want your children to stop manipulative lies and trust you enough to tell you their truths, then you must also be willing to provide an atmosphere that fosters it. You must have a working rapport and understanding with your children. You must, above all, be approachable.

Be that parent your children run to and share their stories with, regardless of the circumstances. In word and action, discipline them without being cruel and wicked, but by being firm and kind. Interact with them without being critical or judgmental. This is how you break the cycle of manipulative lies and deceit, and equally, enjoy the honesty in the conversations and actions of your children.

Meanwhile, I need you to be aware and confident that you have trained your children the best way using the knowledge available to you. Fortunately, you now know better, and you are expected to do better. Peace starts at home and it begins with you.

A Special Note from Abimbola (Peaceful Parent)

Writing a book is more challenging than I thought and more fulfilling than I could have ever imagined.

This book wouldn't have been possible without the full support of my husband, Olakunle. My darling, thank you for your love, your pampering, and your kind gestures during this journey. You will always be my angel.

To my handsome sons, Tantoluwa and Temiloluwa, thank you for your understanding, your emotional support, and your kind words of constant encouragement while writing this book. Mummy loves you both dearly.

I would very much like to thank Omobolanle Abondejo, Amaka Fingesi, Oluwakemi Ogunkoya, Oyinkansola Alabi, and other family members and friends for creating time out of their busy time to contribute to the success of this book. You all have been such a tremendous blessing and encouragement to me.

Also, my heartfelt gratitude goes to My Dad, Chief Joseph Olayiwola Abudiore and Mrs Abosede Abudiore of blessed memory for raising me to be who I am today, being responsible for my existence and putting my foot on a positive and peaceful way of life.

Without the imput of Emmanuel Olatunji, my hardworking, dependable, and amiable publisher, I know this book would remain in my head. It's been a journey of learning and relearning on both sides, but we reached the end. Thank you!

To every organization and individual client that has allowed me to train, coach, or lead in one capacity or the other, I say thank you for believing in me and my organization. The opportunities you have provided have added to my well of experience and equally aided in birthing this book.

Finally, to my maker and the reason for my existence: thank you for my peace of mind, my stability, making peace a source of my strength, for supplying everything I needed to start and finish this book and for giving me the confident hope of a peaceful nation.

I still find it satisfyingly surprising when I see people embrace peaceful parenting. I hope that you understand and accept all I have written in this book and that you evolve into the beautiful parents who raise well-behaved, peaceful, happy, and honest leaders in the future. Thank you so very kindly for investing in my book. I guarantee that you will enjoy this book (and benefit from it) as much as I have.

Dear parents, when there is peace in our hearts, there would be peace in our homes, the nation and the world.

Peace begins with you.

REFERENCES

Koulenti, T. & Anastassiou-Hadjicharalambous, X. (2011). Non-normative life events. In: Goldstein, S., Naglieri, J. A. (eds). Encyclopaedia of child behaviour and development. Boston: Springer. https://doi.org.10.1007/978-0-387-79061-9Koulenti T., Anastassiou-Hadjicharalambous X. (2011) Emotional Connection, Parent-Child. In: Goldstein S., Naglieri J.A. (eds) Encyclopedia of Child Behavior and Development. Springer, Boston, MA. https://doi.org/10.1007/978-0-387-79061-9_985.

Ladd, G. W., & Price, J. M. (1986). Promoting Children's Cognitive and Social Competence: The Relation between Parents' Perceptions of Task Difficulty and Children's Perceived and Actual Competence. Child Development, 57(2), 446–460. https://doi.org/10.1111/j.1467-8624.1986.tb00044.x

Santos, R. M., Zanette, S., Kwok, S. M., Heyman, G. D, & Lee, K. (2017). Exposure to parenting by lying in childhood: Associations with negative outcomes in adulthood. Front Psychol. doi: 10.3389/fpsyg.2017.01900

Serota, K. B. & Levine, T. R. (2015). A few prolific liars: Variation in the prevalence of lying. Journal of Language and Social Psychology. 34:138-157

Talwar, V. & Lee, K. (2008). Social and cognitive correlates of children's lying behaviour. Child Development. 79. 866-81. 10.1111/j.1467-8624.2008.01164.x.).

Xu, F., Bao, X., Fu, G., Talwar, V., & Lee, K. (2010). Lying and Truth-Telling in Children: From Concept to Action. Child Development, 81(2), 581–596. https://doi.org/10.1111/j.1467-8624.2009.01417.x

Made in the USA
Middletown, DE
20 October 2023

41140000R00040